PALESTINIAN

Teenage Refugees and Immigrants Speak Out

IN THEIR OWN VOICES

PALESTINIAN

Teenage Refugees and Immigrants Speak Out

NABIL MARSHOOD

GLOBE FEARON EDUCATIONAL PUBLISHER
A Division of Simon & Schuster
Upper Saddle River, New Jersey

Published in 1997 by The Rosen Publishing Group, Inc.
29 East 21st Street, New York, NY 10010

First Edition
Copyright © 1997 by The Rosen Publishing Group, Inc.

Manufactured in the United States of America.

ISBN 0-835-92233-2

Contents

Palestinian children march on Palestinian Independence Day on November 15, 1994.
On this day, Palestinians celebrate their continuing efforts to achieve independence.

INTRODUCTION

Can you locate Palestine on a world map? You probably will not find it unless you are looking at a map that was printed before 1948. If you have an old map, you can find Palestine on the eastern shore of the Mediterranean Sea. For centuries, this ancient land was known as Palestine. However, since 1948, part of this land has been known as the state of Israel.

What happened in 1948? Who are the Palestinian people, and where are they now? Who are the Israelis? What is the current situation, and what can we say about the future? To answer these and many more questions, we will take a brief journey into the past.

Palestine is the ancient name for an area that is now part of Israel and the Occupied Territories (the Gaza Strip and the West Bank, including east Jerusalem). The region has been inhabited since the dawn of civilization. Its boundaries include the Mediterranean Sea to the west, the Jordan River to the east, Lebanon and Syria to the north, and Egypt to the south.

Palestine is a region rich in religious significance to Jews, Christians, and Muslims alike. Jews claim Palestine as theirs because they believe that it was promised to them by God. Christians believe that Jesus was born, lived, and was resurrected in Palestine. Muslims believe that Muhammad ascended to heaven from Jerusalem, and for that reason Jerusalem is a Muslim holy city.

The name "Palestine" comes from a word meaning "land of the Philistines." Palestinians trace their ancestry to the Canaanites, descendants of Shem, the son of Noah. The Canaanites and the Philistines lived on the coast of Palestine and developed a vibrant economic and cultural life. Important cities such as Jericho, Hebron, Jaffa, and Jerusalem grew up in the region. The Hebrews (Jews) established a kingdom and introduced the Jewish religion to the area. Their kingdom lasted from approximately 1000 B.C. to 586 B.C. They called the region Eretz Israel (Land of Israel). Twelve hundred years later, in 636 A.D., the Arabs conquered Palestine and introduced the Arabic language and the Islamic religion. A Jewish minority remained, but the Jewish population was further reduced when Palestine became a center of Christian pilgrimage in 312 A.D.

Until 1948, Jews in Palestine also considered themselves Palestinians, but today the word "Palestinian" refers only to the Arab Palestinians. Some Palestinians are Muslims, some are Christians, and some belong to other religions. Since the establishment of Israel, most Palestinians live in Israel and the Occupied Territories, while others have left in search of greater freedoms, rights, and opportunities. Many people hope that the continuing peace process will lead to the creation of a Palestinian state.

In 1881 the Zionist movement emerged in Europe. Theodor Herzl, the founder of the World Zionist Organization, wrote *The Jewish State*. Herzl wrote this famous book in response to persistent European anti-Semitism that had long been the cause of discrimination, persecution, and organized massacres known as pogroms. Zionists supported the creation of a separate Jewish state.

Herzl suggested Palestine and several other countries as possible locations for a Jewish state to be established. The idea of a separate Jewish state appealed to many European Jews and led to the first World Zionist Congress, which was held in Basel, Switzerland. Countries such as Argentina, Kenya, Uganda, and Cyprus were also suggested as sites for the Jewish homeland, but the congress decided that Palestine was the ideal

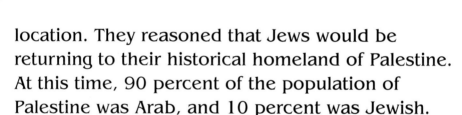

اطلبوا العلم من المهد الى اللحد

ENGLISH TRANSLATION FROM PALESTINIAN ARABIC:
Seek the path of knowledge from the cradle to the grave.

location. They reasoned that Jews would be returning to their historical homeland of Palestine. At this time, 90 percent of the population of Palestine was Arab, and 10 percent was Jewish.

In 1920, after World War I, the League of Nations passed a resolution putting Palestine under British rule. The British began to support Jewish migration to the area in accordance with the 1917 Balfour Declaration. In the Balfour Declaration, the British had pledged their support to help Zionists establish a Jewish homeland in Palestine.

Many Palestinians opposed the Jewish migration and felt that they had been misled by the British. Despite the Balfour Declaration, the British had also promised to help Arab leaders create independent Arab states. The Arabs believed that Palestine was one of the Arab states that would be supported by Britain. However, the British later denied that this had been their intention.

Palestinian efforts to oppose Jewish immigration were put down by either British forces or Jewish militias. In the 1930s, Jewish immigration increased rapidly because of the rise of Adolf Hitler's Nazi Party in Europe. A Palestinian revolt from 1936 to 1939 resulted in the deaths of 5,000 Palestinians and the detention of 10,000 others. In succeeding years, Jewish militant groups carried out acts of terror against Palestinians and at times against the British authorities. Many British, Jewish, and Arab civilians were killed as these groups fought each other for control of Palestine.

When the issue of Palestine was brought before the United Nations (UN) in 1947, the General Assembly voted to split Palestine between the Arab and Jewish peoples. There would be two nations, Israel and Palestine. The United States was among many nations that supported the formation of a Jewish state because of the suffering of the Jewish people during the Holocaust and World War II. In Europe, Hitler's policies had led to the deaths of 6 million Jews.

According to the UN resolution, the Jewish state would be 14,100 square kilometers, consisting of the Negev Desert, the coastal plain between Tel Aviv and Haifa, and part of northern Galilee. The Palestinian state would be 11,100 square kilometers, consisting of the West Bank of the

Jordan River, the Gaza district, and the Arab sector of Galilee. Feeling wronged by the UN—which had allotted the Jewish state 56 percent of the territory, when Jews made up only 35.1 percent of the population and owned only 7 percent of the land—the Palestinians and the neighboring Arab states rejected the partition plan.

On May 14, 1948, the British withdrew from the region. On that same day, the Jewish leadership declared Israel an independent state. Several Arab nations immediately attacked the new state.

By the end of the 1948–1949 war, Israel had taken control of 82 percent of Palestinian territory. Jordan occupied the West Bank and Egypt occupied the Gaza Strip. None of these nations granted the Palestinians the right to self-rule. Approximately 725,000 Palestinians—Muslims and Christians—became refugees as a result of the war. Israel allowed few refugees to return to their homes even after the war. By 1950, over 1 million Palestinians lived in refugee camps. There seemed to be little hope of a new Palestinian state.

After the UN recognized Israel in 1949, relations between Israel and its Arab neighbors entered an intense stage of hostility. In 1956, with the help of Britain and France, Israel invaded Egypt and occupied the Gaza Strip and most of the Egyptian Sinai Peninsula. In an effort to end the violence, UN emergency forces were brought in to maintain a UN cease-fire, and Israel withdrew from the Gaza Strip and the Sinai. In 1967, however, tension built up in the region. Israel launched the Six-Day War against Egypt and Syria; Jordan launched an attack on Israel. After winning the war, Israel controlled the Gaza Strip, the West Bank, the Arab section of east Jerusalem, the Egyptian Sinai, and the Syrian Golan Heights. At least 600,000 more Palestinians became refugees.

Today, about half of all Palestinians live in the Occupied Territories. Since 1967, Palestinians have faced land confiscations, business and travel restrictions, family reunification limits, curfews, and other measures imposed by the Israeli government. Palestinian communities have also been subjected to "collective punishment," in which an entire neighborhood or town is punished for the acts of individuals.

In 1964, Palestinians founded the Palestine Liberation Organization (PLO) at the first Arab summit meeting. The PLO became the only organization to represent Palestinian national aspirations. In its early days, the PLO sponsored terrorist attacks on Israel. But beginning in the early 1970s, the PLO condemned the use of terror. In 1974, the PLO received UN recognition. That same year, the PLO leader, Yasser Arafat, called for the establishment of a democratic and secular state in Palestine where "Christians, Jews, and Muslims live in justice, equality, fraternity and progress." Israel rejected the idea.

In the late 1970s the PLO had bases in Lebanon and sponsored attacks against Israel. For this and other reasons, in 1982, Israel invaded Lebanon. The Israelis destroyed several PLO bases.

Five years later, Palestinians in the Occupied Territories, particularly the youth, began to organize and to demand freedom from Israeli military occupation, which had already lasted for twenty years.

The seven-year uprising that started on December 8, 1987, was known as the Intifada (Arabic for "uprising"). It demanded an end to the Israeli occupation and the creation of a Palestinian state in the West Bank, the Gaza Strip, and east Jerusalem. These three areas constitute less than 20 percent of the territories held by Palestinians prior to 1947. Human rights organizations report that during the first five years of the Intifada (1987–1992), more than 1,000 Palestinians were killed, over 120,000 were injured, and almost 500 were expelled to foreign countries by the Israeli government. Thousands of acres of Palestinian land were confiscated by Israel. More than forty Israelis died in the violence.

It is estimated that during the last fifty years, more than 500 Palestinian villages and towns have been demolished, including cemeteries and places of worship. According to the United Nations, the total number of Palestinian refugees in 1996 was 3.3 million, almost 50 percent of the total Palestinian population. Approximately 33 percent of those refugees live in refugee camps scattered throughout the Middle East. In 1950,

An Israeli soldier watched as two Palestinian children passed his checkpoint in Hebron in October 1996. Israel had ended its curfew in Hebron and had begun to pull its tanks out of the area.

Israel enacted the Law of the Return. According to this law, Jews from all over the world, regardless of their place of birth, may come and live in Israel as full citizens with full legal and human rights. However, this law does not apply to Palestinians.

Israel officially recognized the legitimacy of the PLO in 1992. In September 1993, Israeli Prime Minister Yitzhak Rabin and Palestinian leader Yasser Arafat met in Washington, DC. They signed the first peace agreement to end the conflict. The agreement, known as the Declaration of Principles, stated that Palestinians would form a new political entity. Called the Palestinian National Authority, its members would be elected by the Palestinians, and it would have limited authority to 15

President Bill Clinton oversaw the historic handshake between the late Israeli Prime Minister Yitzhak Rabin and PLO Chairman Yasser Arafat. The handshake followed the signing of the Israeli-PLO peace accord at the White House on September 13, 1993.

rule over certain Palestinian towns and villages in the West Bank and the Gaza Strip. This would not give Palestinians a country of their own but would give them limited self-rule. Two-and-a-half years later on January 20, 1996, Palestinians held their first democratic elections and elected Arafat president of the Palestinian National Authority. According to the Declaration of Principles, a final peace settlement will be negotiated between Israel and the Palestinian people within five years of the Israelis' withdrawal from the Gaza Strip and Jericho area. Many wonder if these agreements will return the Palestinians to their homes.

On November 4, 1995, Rabin was assassinated by a militant Jewish student who opposed the peace agreement. Shimon Peres succeeded Rabin as prime minister. Then, in 1996, Benjamin Netanyahu was elected prime minister.

Many Palestinians are concerned about Netanyahu's rise to power. He has said that he opposes an independent Palestinian state. In August 1996, Netanyahu's government announced plans to expand Jewish settlements in the West Bank and the Gaza Strip. The expansion of settlements has continued despite the condemnation of this policy by the United States, the UN, and the Arab League. Palestinians are angered, and the peace process may be in jeopardy.

In the United States it is difficult to find Palestinian "refugees"; most live in various countries in the Middle East. Most of the interviewees in this book are Palestinians who have recently immigrated to the United States. The level of anxiety among these teenagers is clear. They are afraid of possible retaliation against them or against relatives still living in the Occupied Territories. For this reason, their photographs were not included.

Listen to these Palestinian teens—Muslims and Christians alike. They have much to tell about their experiences as Palestinians in their homeland and in the United States. They have witnessed the tragedy of families and friends losing their homes and land.◆

Lina is sixteen years old. At age seven, she emigrated with her family from Jerusalem, her place of birth, to the United States. She lives in Maryland and plans to study international law. Lina believes that the current Palestinian leadership is not supportive of the Palestinian people and their causes. Her comments were made in response to actions that Yasser Arafat took against Palestinian groups that opposed his regime.

LINA
PEOPLE NEED TO KNOW THE TRUTH

I think that Palestinians should organize themselves better, and that their leaders should work to represent all Palestinians throughout the world. I didn't like it when they closed down universities. Arafat was wrong to arrest Palestinians in the middle of the night because they were suspected of participating in what were called "terrorist activities against Israel." I don't like the way the Palestinian leaders are handling the Palestinian refugees in Lebanon, Jordan, and other places. I don't like how Arafat is presenting the grievances of the Palestinians to the Israeli government and to the rest of the world.

I am very much aware of Palestinian and Zionist history. I know the history of Zionism and the

Palestinian Christians prepare for the Christmas procession in Bethlehem in 1995. The procession goes to the Church of the Nativity, the traditional birthplace of Jesus.

establishment of the state of Israel, and I know that what has happened to the Palestinian people could never have happened to other countries. I think the American government has a double standard. You never hear what happened to the Palestinians. If a Jewish person kills Palestinians—like the Jewish doctor who killed forty Palestinians who were praying in Hebron—he is presented as a madman. However, if a Palestinian does the same to the Israelis, he is called a terrorist, and all Palestinians are punished for what he did. More emphasis is placed on Israeli life than on Palestinian life. What really gets me is that they don't show *why* a young man is willing to kill himself and others. People need to know the truth. People need to understand the main reasons in order to help solve the problem.

The only hope I have is in the Palestinians themselves. I believe that they have to unite and organize themselves. The way it looks today, there are three Palestinian groups: those who live in Israel, those who live in the West Bank and the Gaza Strip, and those who live outside that region. It is not practical for Palestinians from Israel to live under the Palestinian National Authority; they will remain Israeli citizens. Those in the West Bank and the Gaza Strip will be under the rule of the Palestinian Authority, and those outside will be forgotten. As far as the Palestinian refugees are concerned, I do not see much hope for them, but I believe that the Palestinian problem will

A group of Palestinians who were forced to leave Israel and the Occupied Territories in 1992 bow their heads in prayer. These refugees were stranded on the Israeli-Lebanese border when Lebanon rejected Israel's deportation policy and Israel would not allow the men to return home.

never be solved unless the refugee problem is solved.

Although I was born into a Muslim family, I don't see religion as a problem. My family does not practice Islam. I have many friends from all religions, and many of my Christian friends think like me. The Palestinian problem is not religious but political. I am not against Jews or any religion.

I define myself as a Palestinian American and find American teachers to be unsympathetic to the Palestinians. My third-grade sister cried so much when her teacher told her that there is no such thing as Palestine. That made me realize how ignorant many people really are about the subject.

Americans should not believe everything they see on the news. They shouldn't judge the situation before they really understand what is going on.◆

Majeed was born in Jerusalem. He is a nineteen-year-old college student who emigrated with his family two years ago from Ramallah, a town in the West Bank. He lives in Ohio, and he is majoring in political science. Majeed's father was a priest, and his mother worked as a clerk for the city of Ramallah. His family has always been involved with the rest of the Palestinian community in promoting peace.

MAJEED
DEEP ROOTS IN PALESTINE

lived through the Intifada. Since I was twelve years old I lived through the struggle and school closures. Israel closed down the schools and declared education illegal in Palestine. I was never happy with that. Every book, pamphlet, map, or any piece of written information that had the word Palestine on it was banned and confiscated. Every single school, private and public, was closed down, but the students' desire to learn did not stop. We studied secretly. Our parents helped us with our studies. It was dangerous. One day my friend's father was driving us to take an exam in Jerusalem. To get from Ramallah to Jerusalem, a distance of about ten miles, we had to pass through Israeli military checkpoints.

It was very scary. My friend's father asked us to hide our books under the seats because if they were to find our books, they could have arrested us and perhaps put us in jail.

Israeli soldiers used to go into our homes and search for books. To Israel, educating Palestinians was a criminal act and on many occasions has been discouraged. My school in Ramallah is stationed next to the Israeli police station. At times during the Intifada, the Israeli police would fire at us.

As a Palestinian, one can never avoid political involvement. The Intifada gave us the confidence of the new Palestinian age. The Israeli bullets meant nothing to us. The Intifada set the stage for the peace agreement. It actually gave us, the Palestinians, the confidence to speak out and to seek peace.

As a result, in November 1988, the Palestinian National Council (the Palestinian Parliament) met and declared for the first time the establishment of a Palestinian state in exile. We started to know where we were headed. Following that, in September 1993, a peace agreement was signed between Israel and Palestine.

Although I am happy to reach peace, I am not particularly happy with this peace agreement. It divided the Palestinian people into two categories: those who are inside what the agreement defines as Palestine, and those who are outside that territory. It fragmented the Palestinian people and

Palestinian girls look at their new school books as the first school year under limited Palestinian self-rule began on September 1, 1994.

hurt what the Intifada had achieved. This peace was reached gradually, one step at a time. But this is not what we expected. Our culture demands immediacy—we have to see results right away.

Every time we see people shake hands, we think the conflict is over. Many agreements have been reached, but it is not over. The leaders must move toward the final status of a separate Palestinian state. The more they prolong it, the more trouble it will create for both sides. Ramallah, for example, is a small town of about 30,000 people. The West Bank was divided by the 1993 peace accord into three areas: Area A includes seven Palestinian cities, area B includes 405 Palestinian villages, and area C includes all the Israeli settlements on the Palestinian land. Area A is under full control of the Palestinian Authority, area B is under joint security arrangements between Israel and the Palestinian Authority, and area C is under full control of Israel. So for me to visit my friends in different parts of town, I had to go through different security clearances.

Although we haven't seen the fruits of the peace agreement, I am pleased with some of its features. It is good that the education system is now under Palestinian control, and the trend toward an open market economy by the Palestinian Authority is growing.

There are limits to the agreement, however. Many of the Palestinian elite—including highly educated people, businesspeople, professors, and many others—are primarily outside Palestine. These people have been prevented from going back and investing in their country as the Jews have done in Israel. Also, the Palestinian Authority doesn't have control over the crossroads within the country. Going from one part of Palestine to another requires Israeli approval. Even President Arafat must notify the Israelis of his movements within his own country. The Palestinian economy suffers because of all this. Palestinian agricultural products can't be exported to Jordan, for example, without Israeli approval.

How can we develop without adequate means of transportation? Palestinians want to build airports, highways, and businesses, and we want to live in peace, but Israel keeps putting things off, which makes it impossible for us to do the things we want.

Still, I can't lose hope. We live on hope.

Most of my knowledge about Palestine and the history of the conflict is the result of my own research. They don't teach us our history. The word Palestine was never allowed in the textbooks. Legally, on paper, I don't have a nationality. I am a Palestinian, of course, but I carry an Israeli travel document that says that I am Jordanian even though I have never been to Jordan. Those travel documents don't permit me to visit the rest of the Arab countries. Only recently did the Palestinian Authority begin to issue Palestinian passports. I am very happy for that, and I plan to go to Palestine this coming summer to apply and obtain one for myself. Now I am legally Palestinian. The peace agreement of 1993 makes it very clear that Israel—for the first time in history—has acknowledged our existence.

Many people have accepted Palestine as their shelter from oppression. Palestinians are very hospitable people who have opened their doors to different groups throughout history. If you study the origin of the people of Jericho, you will find that they came from Ethiopia. But they settled in Jericho and accepted Palestinian as their nationality. Palestinians have not acted or discriminated against them. We just don't think about these things—they are Palestinians; they are part of us. Also, many Armenians escaped from the Turkish genocide against them and settled in Palestine. They are part of us. They are Palestinians.

I have a hard time understanding Israel. It acts as a nonreligious state, but it is called the Jewish state. Palestinians include Jews, Christians, and Muslims. Palestine has never been a land of one religion. It is difficult to trace the origin of the Palestinian people, but we believe that all of us, including the Jews, came from the Canaanites. There are people who consider themselves Palestinians and who have lived up to the present day in the West Bank. They follow particular Jewish practices. They are called the Samaritans. They have not faced discrimination from the Palestinians. They are Palestinians, and we accept them as part of us.

I am a Christian, but most of my friends in Palestine are Muslims. I reject the statement that the conflict is Palestinian-Jewish. This is wrong. I consider all Palestinians as Israelites.

If it were up to me, I would support the 1974 plan as presented to the United Nations by President Arafat, which calls for the establishment of a secular, democratic state in Palestine where Jews, Christians, and Muslims can live together. Palestine should gain statehood status and have Jerusalem as its capital. Our culture is based on Jerusalem. Jerusalem is a city that defines our identity. I don't accept the partition of Jerusalem.

Hanan Ashrawi served as an adviser and spokeswoman for the Palestinian delegation in the historic Mideast peace talks of 1993. In 1996, Ashrawi won a seat on the Palestinian National Council.

It can be one capital for two states. The eastern part would be the capital of Palestine, and the western side would be the capital of Israel.

I have mixed feelings about immigration to the United States. My parents were born in Palestine, and we have deep roots in that land. There is a fear of losing touch with friends and family. I go back to visit every summer. I don't think I want to settle permanently in the United States, but eventually I want to find a job that would make it possible for me to spend time in both countries. However, with regard to my parents, I hope they go back and retire in Palestine—they were happy there, and they love Palestine.

At times, Americans appear to be uninterested in politics. It seems to me that they have a history of isolationism. The people do not seem to be aware of what the government is doing. Americans tend to think that Palestine and Israel are two countries. They need to understand that the state of Israel was created on the land of Palestine.

Americans need to understand Palestine and the Palestinian people. Referring to someone as a terrorist is not nice. Palestinians are human beings and have been victims of history. Americans need to try to meet Palestinians and learn about the truth.

In addition, Americans need to change their perception of Islam. It is a religion like all other religions of the world, and it deserves to be

Palestinian schoolchildren wave flags and posters to celebrate the arrival of PLO Chairman Yasser Arafat during the 1996 Palestinian elections. Arafat went on to win the presidency.

respected like all other religions. Islam is not a religion of terrorism. Islam might be a new religion here in America. People may have a fear of the unknown. But in order for them to understand, they need to go out there to talk with and meet people of the Islamic faith. Islam is the fastest-growing religion here in America, as well as in Europe. It is important to get out there and open your mind.◆

Nadia is a twenty-year-old college student. She lives in New Jersey and is studying to become a teacher of English literature. Nadia's father, who was born in Deir Debwan, a small town next to Ramallah in the West Bank, is a Muslim. Her mother, born in Brazil, is a Catholic. Nadia lived in the West Bank for ten years, where she went to a private American school.

NADIA
WITNESSING THE INTIFADA

During my years in the West Bank, I witnessed the Intifada firsthand. Palestinian children—Muslims and Christians—went to school together and shared the same experience with the Israeli occupation. During those years, the Palestinian leaders were negotiating with the Israeli leaders over the peace agreement.

During the time of the Intifada, Jewish-Israeli children used to come to our school to discuss their views on the Palestinian issue. They understood us. They were against the Israeli government. We, the Palestinians, were afraid of the outcome of the negotiations between Israeli and Palestinian leaders because the Palestinians had given enough already. It seemed that we were **35**

In 1992, relatives of twelve Palestinians accused of actions against Israel protested an Israeli plan to force the men to leave Israel. The United Nations also disagreed with the Israeli policy of deportation.

being asked to give even more. We did not want the Intifada to be that costly. So many people were killed, imprisoned, or deported. It is wrong for young people to lose their lives.

The Intifada was run by young people. The worst time was when schools were shut down for a year by the Israelis. For the remainder of my school years, school was never "normal" for me or for my friends. One of my friend's cousins was killed. He was actually the first U.S. citizen to be killed in the Intifada. He was about fifteen years old when he was shot by Israeli soldiers. It was horrible. He was missing for a few days before we

found out that he had been killed. We first

received the information while in school. We were shocked. They closed the school. We did not think it could hit so close to home. Knowing the family makes it real. We cried a lot.

Despite all that, we were always optimistic. We were happy even though the Israeli soldiers were shooting at us. They closed our schools and put us under curfew. They killed some of our friends, and others were taken to jail. What kept us happy was our close friendships. We were always there for each other. Our parents did not want us to participate actively in the Intifada. They were concerned for our safety, but we rebelled. I felt I had to do it. This is my duty as a Palestinian. It is part of being connected to the community and its aspiration for freedom and nationhood.

We would go out and demonstrate. I was a little hurt once when a bomb fell near me. It could have killed me. I threw one rock. I was too afraid. I was tear-gassed many times. Once two canisters fell right at my feet and exploded in my face. It was horrible. At the time, though, it seemed normal. It didn't seem to be a bad experience. This is the beauty of being young—you become resilient.

I believed that the Intifada could make a difference, that the world could not stand to see so many people getting killed. But they stood back. Arabs were considered terrorists. Palestinian children fighting for freedom were considered terrorists. Compared with Israeli men and women

The region formerly known as Palestine has many important religious sites. The city of Haifa is the center of the Baha'i religion. The Shrine of the Bab, above, is one of Haifa's best-known landmarks.

soldiers with machine guns, who is more of a terrorist? It is amazing what the Palestinian children have achieved. They fought an army. The Intifada was a revolution of the young people.

This past summer, after the latest peace agreement was signed, I went to visit. There is a feeling of peace—not that Palestinians have everything we want, but there is more of a feeling of personal safety. Walking down the street, you don't have to worry about gunshots or tear-gas bombs. There is definitely hope. Palestinians having their own government gives us hope.

It is important for Americans to understand that Palestinian children are just like any other children of the world. They want to be happy and free, and to grow up in a country they can call their own and be proud of. Wanting that and fighting for it doesn't make them terrorists.◆

Hanna was born in Jerusalem. He is twenty years old. His family is Christian. Three years ago, Hanna came to the United States. He lives in Washington, DC, where he is studying dentistry. His father, a well-known dentist in Ramallah, was recently elected to the parliament of the Palestinian Authority. Hanna has a vision of Palestine becoming a country where people of all religions can live in peace.

HANNA
EVERYBODY WANTS PEACE

I was very proud and hopeful when the first elections were held by the Palestinians in January 1996. The elections were good. People went out to vote, even those who were not supportive of the current peace process. Palestinians voted for candidates who were qualified to run the newly formed government. The Palestinians have chosen the right people for the right positions.

I grew up during the years of the Intifada. For about three years, the Israeli occupation closed down the schools for long periods of time. We realized that this closure would certainly affect our future badly, and so we began looking for alternatives to acquire knowledge. At first we tried to study at home with the help of our parents and relatives, but this did not work. Then we tried to involve the teachers in this process, but we found that this was not successful because the schools were closed for a long time. Finally we organized committees to find local teachers who would conduct classes in our homes. This worked well, and we were able to save our future by getting the knowledge that we need.

The Israeli occupation closed down the schools, claiming that students would use the schools as bases for the activities of the Intifada. But that was not the case. The opposite was true. Schools kept students busy, and therefore they decreased the students' participation in the Intifada. Since education reflects a nation's spirit, the Israeli occupation did not want the Palestinians to be educated. The less educated people are, the easier it is to control them.

During the years of the Intifada, we learned a great deal about Palestine and the conflict with Israel. Almost 70 percent of the current residents of my hometown of Ramallah are originally from the surrounding towns and villages. They were kicked out of their original hometowns in 1948 during and after the first Arab-Israeli war.

I came to the United States about three years ago to study dentistry. After I receive my degree, I plan to return to Palestine, where I intend to practice dentistry and serve my people.

Palestinian women shop for tomatoes in the central market of Ramallah. They were stocking up on supplies after Israel briefly lifted a blockade of West Bank villages in 1996.

In September 1996, Palestinian store owners argue with Israeli soldiers who refused them entry to the Jewish settlement in Hebron. Jewish settlers seized two Palestinian-owned stores and made them part of the settlement.

I came to study in the United States because I am fluent in the English language and I have relatives who immigrated to America a long time ago. Actually, about 90 percent of the original residents of Ramallah live in the United States. Also, there is no medical or dental school in Palestine; the Israelis have them, but Palestinians are not allowed in.

The Palestinian Authority began to build a new medical school in Jerusalem, right in the heart of the Holy Land. I am very happy about that. Finally, we are allowed to do what is going to benefit all the people in the region, including Jews.

My friends are of all religions—Christians, Muslims, and Jews. Religion has never been a problem in Palestine. It has always seemed to me that the conflict has been political, not religious. Actually, before the start of the conflict, Muslims, Christians, and Jews lived together in Palestine. My grandfather used to tell me that they never had a problem. He told me stories about his many Jewish friends. He said that they used to visit with each other and work together, and even participate in each other's religious celebrations. People were living together, and everything was fine. However, after 1948, all communications between them were cut. That is a terrible thing.

I hope peace will come back again, but it will take time. The hatred that grew on both sides for the last fifty years is not going to dissolve right away. A few weeks ago, I saw one Israeli man on television saying that President Arafat should keep his animals in their cage. This man used the term "animals" to refer to Palestinians and the term "cage" to refer to the Gaza Strip. Changing such attitudes is going to take some time. I certainly want peace. Everybody wants peace, and I am optimistic about the situation.

The Palestinian refugees are still there. It is a complex subject. These people were kicked off of their land, and they lost their properties. They should be allowed to return to their homes and be compensated for what they have lost. However, at least at the present time, this is unlikely to happen.

Many of the American people are not familiar with the reality of the Palestinian problem. Before making any judgment, especially about the Middle East, they need to listen to both sides of the story. In general, most Americans develop their views on the Arab-Israeli conflict from information they get from the American media, which are known to be supportive of Israel. The media don't usually explain the suffering of the Palestinian people that has been going on for the last fifty years.

I believe that people in the Holy Land should work for peace. The Palestinians have suffered so much from this conflict. Many people have been killed. Many have been wounded, and many have been imprisoned by the Israelis. It is time to stop that. Every Palestinian has paid a heavy price in order to achieve our national goal, which is to create a democratic secular Palestinian state. I am glad we have started.◆

Mohammed is eighteen years old. He was born in Saudi Arabia. His father is Palestinian, and his mother is Syrian. Mohammed's father, a physician, was born in Ramla—a small town next to Lod between Jerusalem and Tel Aviv. Mohammed has never visited Palestine, but he considers himself Palestinian as well as Saudi Arabian. He came to the United States to study medicine and lives in Washington, DC.

MOHAMMED
I FEEL PALESTINIAN

My name is Mohammed. I am aware of the latest peace agreement between Palestine and Israel. Peace is good. Palestinians have somewhere they can call home. They have a country now. It is a small country. I wish they could make it bigger. Every Palestinian has that wish.

I also wish I could visit Palestine. I am not allowed to visit because there are no agreements between Saudi Arabia and Israel that would permit such visits. I have a strong desire to visit the ancient and historic town of Jerusalem and the A1-Aqsa mosque located in the heart of Jerusalem. The A1-Aqsa mosque is one of the holiest sites in Islam. Actually, I wish I could visit all the holy sites in Jerusalem, particularly the ones holy to Muslims. I saw pictures of them. I think they are beautiful.

I do not know all the details about Palestine, but I know enough, and I feel Palestinian. The seven-year Intifada that started around 1988 was a great thing. Palestinians finally realized that they were oppressed. The Intifada was a natural development. I used to watch the events on television. Palestinians are really brave. They were able to stand in front of Israeli soldiers. They were alone, armed with stones, facing an army with all its power. There were times when I wondered what I would have done if I were in their place. I felt sorry that I could not help. I cried.

In high school in Saudi Arabia, we were taught about the Arab-Israeli wars and the Palestinian crisis. It all started with the war of 1948. The state of Israel was established, and as a result Palestine was dismantled. Palestine was given away by the British to the Jews. As a result, Palestinians were left without a country. Some ran away because they did not want to stay under Israeli rule, some stayed in their homes, some were killed, and some were forced to leave. This is not fair. Jews claim that Palestine belongs to them historically,

Palestinian schoolboys in the town of Jenin walk along a street decorated with Palestinian flags.

Palestinian schoolgirls hold anti-violence signs in a March 1996 demonstration against bombings carried out in Israel by the group Hamas.

but it is not true. I never paid attention to politics before, but now I do.

America is a good country, but once I am done with my education, I plan to return to Saudi Arabia.

I do not think I will live long enough to see Palestine the way it used to be. The current Palestine is not complete. I don't think Palestinians and Jews can ever live in peace after all the killing. I would tell the Palestinians to be patient—Palestine will be back. We were taught in school in Saudi Arabia that Palestine must be in Muslim hands. Christians can live there, and the Jews may stay or go back to the places they came from. I think that Palestine should be a Muslim country. I hope this will bring peace; maybe then Jews will understand.

I have both Muslim and Christian but not Jewish friends, because I was never introduced to a Jewish person. I am not a racist. Jews are nice people.

Now I live in Washington, DC. I am happy here, but I notice that Americans do not know about the Arabs. I want to tell them that Arabs are a big population. Americans should not generalize. Not all Arabs are terrorists. Many movies show negative images of Arabs. Remember the Oklahoma bombing? People first thought, without investigation, that it was carried out by an Arab. They were wrong. It was carried out by a non-Arab American. I think Americans have to know the facts about the Arabs and meet with more Arab people.◆

Rana is sixteen years old. She is the middle child of a Palestinian family that immigrated to the United States in 1987. Rana lives with her family in Maryland. Her parents were born in Palestine but grew up in Jordan. Today Rana and her father, unlike her mother and brother, have no permission from the Israeli government to visit their family in the Palestinian territories. Rana is waiting to obtain her American citizenship so she can visit the rest of her family in Palestine.

6 RANA
A DOUBLE LIFE

I have a lot of family in Palestine. I don't know them, but I'd like to know them. I feel I have lost something because I don't know my full origin. Why can't I go and visit my own country? It seems wrong that I have to become an American to be able to do so—it is like leading a double life.

I know the basic "stuff" about the history of Palestine. Maybe I should know more, but I know the history of how Israel was established on Palestinian land and that the Palestinian people had to leave. I believe that wars don't solve the problem, but I wish the Jews would just leave my country. I want to see my country restored. Even though this will never happen, one can never give

Ghada Karmi and Ellen Siegel stand in protest in front of the Israeli embassy in London in 1992. Their signs refer to Israel's Law of the Return.

up hope. I define myself as a Palestinian Arab. I dream of my country being free. Maybe Arab unity could lead to this, but this is also unrealistic. I want the Jews out of my country. They are splitting the Arab world and taking control of the Arab nations as well. Palestinians and Israelis will never live happily together. The peace treaty that was signed between Arafat and the Israelis is just a piece of paper that the people don't really want. Nobody is happy unless they get what they want. Both Israelis and Palestinians want the other out.

I am very critical of Israel, but I am also critical of Mr. Arafat and his actions. I feel that he is selling his people out—he doesn't care. My father thinks that Arafat is a puppet for the Israelis, and I agree with him. He does what he is told, not what is right and not what the majority want him to do.

I live in a Jewish community and I have many Jewish friends. They know my position, so we avoid talking about the subject. I can't blame all Jews for the problem. I can't hate or judge them because they are Jews. One of my best friends is a Jew. I am very picky with my friends. I have many Christian friends, and some of my friends lately have been non-Arab Muslims. We get along well.

At times I consider myself a refugee. All Palestinians are refugees. We can't go back to our country. What really gets me is that the world finds it necessary for the Israelis to have a country. Why don't the Palestinians get or deserve one? I feel there is not much hope. Whatever happens, happens. I don't think it will be good. A part of me is missing. Until the dream comes true it will remain missing. To find some answers for myself, I intend to participate in a Palestinian-American camp this coming summer.

One of my dreams, since I was four years old, has been to become a dentist. I feel that this is what is good about America: Everyone has a chance to go to college, and people can achieve their dreams.

I want all Americans to know the truth about Palestine and the Palestinians. Americans shouldn't look at the cause from just one perspective. They don't see what happens to the

These Israeli soldiers are stationed in a section of Jerusalem's Old City, where many of the Arab residents of Jerusalem live.

Palestinians and their children. They don't understand what we go through. They think we are bad
people. We are not! I wish they understood this. I
think that with information, some people may
change their minds and become aware of the
Palestinians' condition, but the Israelis put a ban
on information. I once watched a videotape in
which the Israelis were beating Palestinian
children on their heads. I know that people here
in America don't see this.◆

Glossary

anti-Semitism Hostility toward or discrimination against Jews. The term "Semite" refers to the peoples believed to be descended from Shem, son of Noah. Arabs are also Semites.

British Mandate The placement of Palestine under British control by the League of Nations in 1922.

Canaanites A people who inhabited Palestine from approximately 3000 B.C.

genocide The intentional and systematic killing of an entire people or national group.

Intifada Arabic for "uprising." A seven-year political revolt carried out by young Palestinians against the Israeli occupation.

Islam A religion that holds that Allah is the one God. The teachings of Islam are found in the

Koran (Quran), which Muslims believe was revealed to Muhammad.

isolationism A policy of avoiding political alliances and relations.

League of Nations The body that preceded the United Nations.

Palestine Ancient name for what is today Israel and the Occupied Territories. Today the word "Palestinian" refers to the Arab Palestinians, be they Muslim or Christian and whether they live in Palestine or not.

Palestine Liberation Organization (PLO) National political movement of the Palestinian people founded in 1964.

Palestinian National Authority (PNA) A political entity representing certain towns and villages in the West Bank and the Gaza Strip.

Palestinian National Council The parliament of the Palestinian National Authority. Before the establishment of the Palestinian National Authority, this body was the Palestinian council in exile representing Palestinian interests.

Philistines A people who came to Palestine in approximately 1300 B.C.

resilient Able to recover and adjust easily.

sovereignty Supreme and independent political authority.

Zionism Jewish political movement founded by Theodor Herzl in 1881 in response to persistent European anti-Semitism.

For Further Reading

Dudley, William, ed. *The Middle East.* San Diego, CA: Greenhaven Press, 1992.

Greenberg, Keith. *Gaza: Struggle for a Mideast Homeland.* Woodbridge, CT: Blackbirch Press, 1996.

Haskins, James. *Leaders of the Middle East.* Hillside, NJ: Enslow Publishers, 1985.

Steins, Richard. *The Mideast After the Gulf War.* Brookfield, CT: Millbrook Press, 1992.

Challenging Reading

Abu-Ghazaleh, Adnan. *History and Culture of the Ancient Middle East and North Africa.* Brattleboro, VT: Amana Books, 1991.

Morris, B. *The Birth of the Palestinian Refugee Problem.* New York: Cambridge University Press, 1987.

Said, Edward. *The Question of Palestine.* New York: Times Books, 1980.

Stockton, Ronald. *The Israeli-Palestinian Conflict: A Unit for High School Students.* Ann Arbor: University of Michigan Center for Middle Eastern and North African Studies, 1993.

Index

About the Author

Nabil Marshood is of Palestinian heritage and was born and raised in Israel. He is a professor of social sciences and human services at Hudson County Community College in New Jersey. He received his doctorate in social work from Columbia University. He has published many articles and research papers.

Photo Credits

Cover by Ira Fox; pp. 6, 15, 18, 22, 31, 36, 40, 51, 52, 58, © AP/Wide World Photos; p. 16, © Reuters/Gary Hershorn/Archive Photos; pp. 20, 34, 48, 54, © Reuters/Jim Hollander/Archive Photos; pp. 24, 44, © Reuters/David Silverman/Archive Photos; p. 27, © Reuters/Nati Shohat-Flash 90/Archive Photos; pp. 33, 43, © Reuters/Rula Halawani/Archive Photos; p. 38, © Johnny Stockshooter/International Stock; p. 56, courtesy of Ellen Siegel.

Layout and Design

Kim Sonsky